PUNISHMENT IN DERBYSHIRE

BY

JOHN N. MERRILL

Map and photographs by John N. Merrill

a J.N.M. PUBLICATION

1988

i

a J.N.M. PUBLICATION

JNM PUBLICATIONS,
WINSTER,
MATLOCK,
DERBYSHIRE.
DE4 2DQ

Conceived, edited, typeset, designed, marketed and distributed by John N. Merrill.

© Text — John N. Merrill 1987

© Map, sketches and photographs — John N. Merrill 1987

First Published — January 1988

ISBN 0 907496 33 4

Meticulous research has been undertaken to ensure that this publication is highly accurate at the time of going to press. The publishers, however, cannot be held responsible for alterations, errors or omissions, but they would welcome notification of such for future editions.

Set in Rockwell, medium and bold.

Printed by: Linprint, Mansfield, Nottinghamshire.

ABOUT JOHN N. MERRILL

John combines the characteristics and strength of a mountain climber with the stamina and athletic capabilities of a marathon runner. In this respect he is unique and has to his credit a whole string of remarkable long walks. He is without question the world's leading marathon walker.

Over the last ten years he has walked more than 60,000 miles and successfully completed ten walks of at least 1,000 miles or more.

His six major walks in Great Britain are —
Hebridean Journey .... 1,003 miles
Northern Isles Journey .... 913 miles
Irish Island Journey .... 1,578 miles
Parkland Journey .... 2,043 miles
Lands End to John o'Groats .... 1,608 miles
and in 1978 he became the first person (permanent Guinness Book of Records entry) to walk the entire coastline of Britain — 6,824 miles in ten months.

In Europe he has walked across Austria — 712 miles — hiked the Tour of Mont Blanc, completed High Level Routes in the Dolomites, and the GR20 route across Corsica in training! In 1982 he walked across Europe — 2,806 miles in 107 days — crossing seven countries, the Swiss and French Alps and the complete Pyrennean chain — the hardest and longest mountain walk in Europe, with more than 600,000 feet of ascent!

In America he used the the world's longest footpath — The Appalachian Trail —2,200 miles — as a training walk. He has walked from Mexico to Canada via the Pacific Crest Trail in record time — 118 days for 2,700 miles.

During the summer of 1984, John set off from Virginia Beach on the Atlantic coast, and walked 4,226 miles without a rest day, across the width of America to Santa Cruz and San Francisco on the Pacific Ocean. His walk is unquestionably his greatest achievement, being, in modern history, the longest, hardest crossing of the USA in the shortest time — under six months (178 days). The direct distance is 2,800 miles.

Between major walks John is out training in his own area — the Peak District National Park. As well as walking in other parts of Britain and Europe he has been trekking in the Himalayas five times. He has created more than ten challenge walks which have been used to raise more than £250,000 for charity. From his own walks he raised over £80,000. He is author of more than eighty books, most of which he publishes himself. His book sales are in excess of 2 million. His next major walk — 2.400 miles — is down the length of New Zealand.

CONTENTS

WORMHILL STOCKS

INTRODUCTION

In a macbre way I have been fascinated by the punishments and sentences of the last few centuries. From seeing village stocks and reading stories about people in pillories or being executed, I began researching to learn more about this side of life. The Padley Martyrs of 1588 are well known, so too is the fate of the ring leaders of the Pentrich Rebellion in 1817. I began researching in the various local history libraries in Sheffield, Chesterfield and Derby uncovering snippets and leads to this absorbing subject! Slowly I pieced together the information and went out on location to see the site where a murder or ducking stool took place. It made my walking fascinating.

My aim has simply been to generally describe the various forms of punishemnt, starting with the mildest. Then progressing with the more severe and climaxing on the most brutal. Thankfully they are all part of the past. Many sites and features can be seen today and these are detailed in the sections. I hope they give you added insight into life a couple of centuries ago, as well making exploring the county more interesting!

Happy exploring!

John N. Merrill.

John N. Merrill
Winster. November 1987.

1

UPPERTOWN STOCKS, Nr. BIRCHOVER

LITTLE LONGSTONE STOCKS

EYAM HALL AND STOCKS

STOCKS

Although used in Roman times, it was not until Edward the Third in 1351 passed an Act for stocks to be placed in every town that this form of punishment was used in England. At first they were used for people who would not take an oath to observe the law, but were later used principally for drunkards and disturbers of the peace. Many stocks can still be seen in Derbyshire, such as at Chapel-en-le-Frith, Wormhill, Little Longstone, Eyam, Upper Town just south of Birchover and Sudbury. In Warslow just inside Staffordshire above the Manifold Valley are some metal stocks.

Henry the Seventh passed an Act in 1496 — "It is enacted that vagabonds, idle and suspected persons, shall be set in the stocks three days and three nights, and have none other sustenance than bread and water, and then shall be put out of the town." If it was a second offence, you were in the stocks for six days and six nights. Henry the Eighth curtailed the punishment in 1504, when the offenders were placed in the stocks for only one day and night. Later still the punishment was reduced further. An Act of 1624 stated that one either paid a fine of 1/- (5p) or spent three hours in the stocks.

Being placed in the stocks was a humiliating affair. Written in 1894 -

"The culprit was securely locked in the stocks. How ludicrous he looked, jeered at and taunted by the passers-by, the laughing stock of the lads and the disgust of his friends!"

By the beginning of the nineteenth Century, stocks were starting to go into disuse. 1829 is believed to be the last year when they were used in Derbyshire. Fairey wrote in his "General View of the Agriculture of Derbyshire", which was published in 1815 -

"Sitting in the Parish of Township stocks, a summary and wholesome manner of paying for the less heinous offences against good morals, seems here, and almost everywhere else, to have gone into entire disuse; although, ridiculously enough, every country place continues religiously to uphold its stocks. On a great many occasions when seeing them repairing, or new ones erecting, and such as lately had been renewed, I have enquired whether anyone in their place remembered a single instance of the stocks being used; but have invariably, except by very old persons, been answered in the negative."

In November 1651, Richard Dakin from Ashover was sentenced to occupy the stocks —

"This informant sayth that upon Friday night beeing the fourteenth day of this instant November Richard Dakin, of Ashover, gentleman, beeing far gone in drinks, and quarrelling with the said William Hiberd, swore twenty severall oathes and was very much debeysted other wayes."

WARSLOW STOCKS

4

PILLORIES

After being in the pillory, a writer wrote —

"The storm commenced. Stones began to spit, mud to mizzle, cabbage stalks thickened into a shower. Now and then a dead kitten — sometimes a living cat; anon an egg would hit me on the eye, an offence I was obliged to wink at. There is a strange appetite in human kind for pelting a fellow creature."

The pillory was a popular form of punishment in the 18th Century. Similar in design to the stocks, but instead of having your feet clasped between boards you had your head and hands, and because of this it was often referred to as the "stretch neck". The main occupiers of the pillory were bakers or butchers who had sold food underweight. But persons about to serve a prison sentence were frequently placed in the pillory to start with. For example —

"1736 — April 1s. Lent Assizes. George Lomas, for forging the hands of Thomas Cheetham and Richard Bagshaw, Esqrs., to a certificate, to stand in the pillory at Tideswell one hour and to be imprisoned six months."

When you were placed in the pillory you were powerless. The locals used you for target practice, using rotten fruit and vegetables as missiles. Many of the towns of Derbyshire had a pillory, and there was recorded in 1330 — "The proprietors of the Manor of Repton claimed to be Lords of the Hundred, and to have within their manor a pillory, tumbrell, and gallows, for the punishment of criminals."

Following 1816 the only criminals to be placed in the pillory were perjury cases. The use of the pillory was abolished on June 30th 1837,

In Ashby de la Zouch church, in Leicestershire, is a finger pillory, used to subdue the unruly in church! It comprises of two posts supporting a beam with thirteen grooves of varying sizes to match the thickness of different culprit's fingers.

FINGER PILLORY IN ST. HELEN'S CHURCH, ASHBY DE LA ZOUCH

WHIPPING

For minor offences this was a popular form of punishment, from the mediaeval days. Very often the stocks were made with a tall post so that the male or female would be fastened to it and there publicly whipped. Sometimes the pillory was used as the whipping post. It was not until a statute of 1791 that females were no longer whipped. The whipping of males continued right on into this century.

A typical entry from the Order of Sessions —

"1691 — Wheras Thomas Carlile als carelesse and William
Ward stand convicted of Petit Larceny at this Sessions
it is Ordered by this Cort that they bee carryed back
to the County Gaole and that on Fryday the twenty fourth
of this instant Apll the Sherriffe of this county cause
them to bee stripped to the wast and whipt till bloody in
the height of the market at Derby and then remanded to
the said Gaole and on Ashbourne Faireday next to bee stript
to the wast and whipt till bloody in the height of the said
Faire in Ashbourne and afterwards to bee delivered to the
master of the House of Correction in Derby there to be kept
until the next Quarter Sessions of the Peace and that they
have noe allowance during their stay there but what they
shall earne by their labour."

Another entry records that on 29th September 1738 Alice Peason, an unmarried woman, confessed to stealing — "the cloth belonging to the coach seat being the property of Bach Thornhill Esqr." She was tried in Chesterfield, and the Justice wrote on the sentence — "She is a Yorkshire woman. I hope she will be severly whipd at Chesterfield and sent home."

No whipping posts can be seen in Derbyshire today, but closeby at Greatgate near Alton above the Churnet Valley in Staffordshire, is a stone whipping post.

WHIPPING POST, GREATGATE NR ALTON

HOUSES OF CORRECTION

Following the dissolution of the monasteries in 1539, the term "House of Correction" came to be used. It was not until the early 17th Century that, during Elizabeth the First's reign, legislation was passed stating that all shires were to have at least one House of Correction for "rogues, vagabonds and sturdy beggars". At first there were three, at Ashbourne, Chesterfield and Derby. A further two were later built at Tideswell and Wirksworth. Their use extends over two centuries, and it was not until the Poor Law Amendment Act of 1834 and the Police Act of 1839 that the Houses of Correction were abandoned, and gaols in the police stations were used for such people.

ASHBOURNE

Not known when first built, but the date of the earliest petition from the House is dated 1660. The keeper of a House of Correction generally administered the punishments sentenced by the Justices. In 1719 —

"A sheepstealer was ordered by the Justices to be whipped in open market at Ashbourne in the forenoon and at Doveridge in the afternoon; and for quelling any disturbance that might be attempted by his relatives or confederates, the keeper of the Ashbourne House of Correction, who was to administer the punishment, was to take with him the late Act of Parliament for quelling riots, and to publicly read it before each flogging."

In 1722, at the Epiphany Sessions, it was decided to build a new House of Correction, but it was not until 1815 that the building was completed at a cost of £2,252.5s.11d. (£2,252.30p). The keeper in 1765 was Thomas Litton Jnr., who received a salary of £15 per year. In 1817 the salary was £50.

CHESTERFIELD

"The building was erected in 1614, in a low, damp situation, on the bank of the River Hipper, the worst place that could be found for such a purpose. It is under the superintendence of the Magistrates of the Hundred of Scarsdale."

It also served the High Peak Hundred as well, until Tideswell's House of Correction was built in 1711. In 1741 the Chesterfield House of Correction was closed, and the keeper was given an annual salary of £10. Three years later the House was re-opened. In 1815 approximately £550 was spent on the House, and in 1820 a surgeon was appointed with a salary of £20.

DERBY

Originally the House of Correction was located in Walker Lane, but in 1756 the House of Correction and County Gaol were placed under the same roof. In 1695, instead of having a male as a keeper, a female was given the post. A typical sentence for being placed in the House of Correction is as follows:-

"1719. Mich. Sessions. Grace Rowe, who stole a gown,
is committed to the Derby House of Correction and to be
kept to hard labour and severely punished in such manner
and as often as the Master thereof shall think fitt."

TIDESWELL

Order of the Easter and Trans. Sessions, 1711.

"The poore and punishment of vagrants and idle dissolute
persons for want of some convenient Prison Gaole or House
of Correction for ye punishment of such like persons it
was this day ordered and this Court doth order that a
House of Correction shall be erected and established at
Tideswell in this county, and that William Shore of
Tideswell aforesaid shall be, and is hereby appointed,
Master or Keeper of the same and shall immediately enter
on the said office."

Following the Vagrant Act of 1739, the Houses of Correction became filled with
tramps, which meant very little room for everyone. In Tideswell a vagrant was
allotted a space 6½ ft. by 5 ft. 7 ins.. There were as many as twenty a night in
Tideswell. The Keeper complained in 1741, but it was not until 1816 that a new one
was built at a cost of over £600. In 1827, a pew was made for the Church for
prisoners from the House of Correction at a cost of £6.12s.0d. (£6.60p).

WIRKSWORTH

There was a House of Correction here in about 1670, but it was later abandoned. In
about 1720 a petition was made to the Quarter Sessions asking for a House of
Correction.

"That Wirksworth is a very populous place and greatly
oppressed with poor by reason of the mines now in
decay. . . "

A House of Correction was re-established here in 1727.

DOG BITING

At the Derby Assizes of 1716, William Foxlow of Tideswell, who was a fellmonger, was fined 12s.8d (63p) and had to pay £8.7s.0d. (£8.35p) compensation for —

"Keeping a great mastiff dog, and suffering it to go loose, and being unmuzzled, by which means it hath done great injuries to Edward Palfreman who hath been bitten."

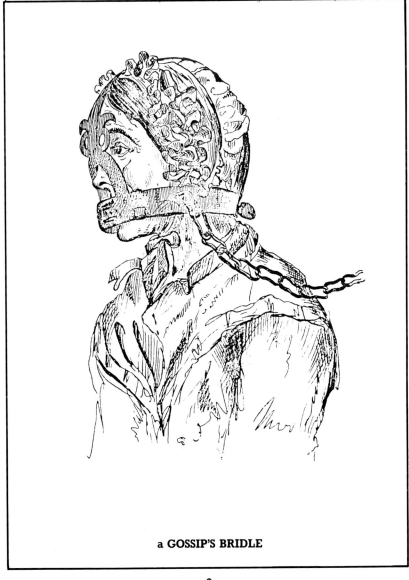

a GOSSIP'S BRIDLE

THE GOSSIP'S BRIDLE

Sentence — "That it is the unaminous decision of the Mayor and Justices that the prisoner. . . . ., there and then have the Town's Bridle for Scolding women put upon her, and that she be led by the Magistrates' Clerk's Clerk through every street in the town, as an example to all scolding women."

Scolding women were described as — "Troublesome and angry woman who by brawling and wrangling amongst her neighbours, breaks the public peace, increases discord, and becomes a public nuisance to the neighbourhood."

Another punishment for women, principally for scolding women. Often it is referred to as the Brank or Scold's Bridle. It became a popular form of punishment in the 17th Century, although never legalised, Derbyshire women were described as being very loyal and not ones for spreading slander, and this would appear to be true, for only one "bridle" is known. This was made in Chesterfield in 1688, the year of the Glorious Revolution, and is still in existence, although privately owned. One can be seen in Derby Museum. A bridle is described as being as follows:-

"It consisted of a kind of crown, or framework of iron,
was locked upon the head, and was armed in front with
a gag, a plate, or a sharp cutting knife or point,
which was placed in the poor woman's mouth, so as to
prevent her moving her tongue — or, it was so placed
that if she did move it, or attempted to speak, it was
cut in a most frightful manner. With the cage upon
her head, and with the gag firmly pressed and locked
against her tongue, the miserable creature, whose sole
offending perhaps was that she had raised her voice in
defence of her social rights against a brutal and besotted
husband, or had spoken honest truth of someone high in
office in her town, was paraded through the streets, led
by a chain by the hand of the bell-man, the beadle or the
constable; or chained to the pillory, the whipping-post
or market cross, to be subjected to every conceivable
insult and degradation, without even the power left her
of asking for mercy, or of promising amendment for the
future — and, when the punishment was over, she was
turned out from the Town Hall, or the place where the
brutal punishment had been inflicted, maimed, disfigured,
bleeding, faint and degraded, to be the subject of
comment and jeering amongst her neighbours, and to be
reviled at by her persecutors."

From, "Old and New Chesterfield", Tatler 1889.

THE DUCKING STOOL

A Ducking Stool is described as -

"A post was set up in a pond; across this post was placed
a transverse beam, turning on a swivel with a chair at
one end, in which, when the culprit was properly placed,
that end was turned to the pond and let into the water;
and this was repeated as often as the virulence of the
distemper required."

The ducking stool was used basically for brawling and scolding women, and was
in use from about 1560 to the mid-1700s. The last known usage was in Rugby in
1750 by a man for beating his wife. The one in Nottingham was last used in 1731
and on this occasion the woman died from the ducking, due to the over zealous
crowd!

The one in Chesterfield, which was placed over Silk Mill Dam, was taken down in
1790. The lord of the manor usually passed sentence on the offending woman, and,
depending on her crime, decided the number of duckings she would receive. On
average it was three. Other Derbyshire ducking stools are known to have existed
at Alfreton, Ashbourne, Belper, Melbourne and Wirksworth.

"Down in the deep the stool descends,
But here, at first, we miss our ends,
She mounts again, and ranges more,
Than ever vixen did before;
So throwing water on the fire,
Will make it burn up the higher,
If so, my friends, pray let her take
A second turn into the lake;
And rather than your patient lose,
Thrice and again repeat the dose;
No brawling wives, no furious wenches,
No fire so hot but water quenches."

In West's poem, published 1780.

11

SMISBY LOCK-UP

ALFRETON LOCK-UP

LOCK-UPS

Littered along the boundary of Derbyshire and Leicestershire are several small circular buildings, known as Lock-Ups. Two on the Derbyshire side can been seen in Ticknall and Smisby. The one in Ticknall village, on the main street with its spire roof, is a particularly splendid example. Just inside Leicestershire, others can be seen — Breedon, Worthington and Packington. It would seem that these lock-ups were made to replace stocks and were occupied by both drunkards and brawlers. Occasionally they were used as overnight accomodation when transporting prisoners.

On the main street in Alfeton, almost unnoticed is a two roomed lockup with circular windows. It was built in 1815 and inscribed over the door — "House of Confinement." Another is opposite the Bluebell Inn at Sandiacre and incorporates a pinfold and was built about 1660.

Very little is known about them, but an amusing true tale exists concerning the Ticknall lock-up which occurred last century. Living in the village was Mrs. Soar who, although ninety years of age, kept the Loaf and Cheese public house. She had lived there for seventy years, and could tell many a tale about the village. One year, at the Annual Wakes held in July, several people were rather boisterous and a little worse for drink. Although a good hundred were in such a state, only ten were locked up in the small round house. A few months before, Mrs. Soar had found out, quite by accident, that her kitchen door key fitted the lock of the lock-up. When everyone was in bed and the ten inside the lock-up were moaning of their fate and cramped conditions, Mrs. Soar slipped out and headed for the lock-up. Once she had persuaded the occupants to be quiet and not to tell a soul, she undid the door and let them out. Next morning the cart and constable came to the lock-up, watched by a large crowd and Mrs. Soar. The constable unlocked the door, and to his amazement found the lock-up was empty. It was not until many years later that Mrs. Soar told of her part in the story.

13

PINFOLD AND LOCKUP, SANDIACRE

DEBTORS

A debtor's life in either a House of Correction or prison was one of the saddest fates that men in the 17th and 18th Centuries could experience. If you had no friend to bail you out and settle your debts, then your future was extremely grim. Extract from a letter dated 25th November 1690 from Chesterfield's House of Correction:-

"Into close prison he must be clapt, and if he have no
money wherewith to help himself withal, he may starve
for want of sustenance, for no relief at all will be
afforded him, neither by the Town nor by the gaoler;
and if the Prisoners make any complaint, all that is
said in excuse is, if any allowance should be afforded
them, they would never pay their debts, and so the poor
prisoners may starve for want."

In about 1790, there was a gaol for debtors under Chesterfield's Town hall.

THE COUNTY GAOL

"For a new jail to be made within the County of Derby,
in like form as is afore provised for other shires
aforesaid."

The above is an extract from the Act of 1532 stating that a gaol was to be built in Derby. Before this date, and until the gaol was built, prisoners from Derbyshire were imprisoned in Nottingham. In 1566 each county had its own Sheriff, but it was not until 1588, over fifty years after the Act, that Derbyshire had its own County Gaol. The Gaol was placed in the most inhospitable place imaginable and was renowned "for its foulness and consequent frequest visitations of plague and gaol fever". It was built in the Corn Market, over the then open brook, which was at that time the town's sewer. It is recorded that in 1610 the brook rose suddenly and three prisoners were drowned.

Bread was provided for all prisoners out of public funds. In 1682 the prisoners wrote a petition to the Justices complaining of the quality of the bread supplied by the new baker: "His bread was not soe wholsome and servicable as that which former bakers have delivered." The Justices decided that the new and old bakers should provide the bread on alternate weeks. Nine years later in 1691 at the Michaelmas Sessions it was — "Ordered that the prisoners' allowance of 1½d. (1p) per day be reduced to the allowance of one penny (½p) per day till further order in regard to the cheapness of Corne". At the Epiphany Sessions, the allowance reverted back to 1½d. (1p) because of the "dearnesse of Corne".

SOME KEY DATES —

1718 — Gaol beds were repaired.

1719 — A prisoner escaped through a window into the Corn Market. . . and the Court ordered that the window was to be sealed up immediately.

1732 — Mrs. Mary Greatorex, widow, was made the gaoler.

1752 — On 13th February four prisoners escaped through a hole in the wall which they had made. Three were never caught, but the fourth, Anthony Frost, returned back through the hole the next morning.

1756 — A new gaol was built at Friar's Gate, and was made to hold twenty-one criminals and twenty-six debtors. However, as recorded later, this was hopelessly small, as sixty years later three times that number occupied the gaol.

1762 — Blyth Simpson, who was both the gaoler to the felons and debtors as well as Keeper of the House of Correction, received an annual salary of £60.

1764 — A law was passed that — "No gaoler is to suffer tippling or gaming in the prison, or to sell any liquors therein, under the penalty of £10 to be recovered by distress upon conviction." Prior to this law, the gaoler made a very good living from selling alcohol to the prisoners, as much as double his salary. Consequently he was given an extra £120 on top of his salary — "A year's increase of salary on account of his not being allowed to sell ale."

1774 — Following an Act passed regarding the health and condition of prisoners and gaols, a bath was fitted in the gaol. A surgeon was appointed — John Harrison — at a salary of £30. The prison was also annually whitewashed and scraped, and eight guineas (£8.40p) was allotted to provide new straw for the inmates.

1793 — The gaoler received an annual salary of £200.

1820 — The gaol was bursting with inmates, as there were 69 people imprisoned. Two years later, in 1822, it was decided to purchase six acres of land near the Uttoxeter road. The cost of building a new gaol was estimated at £37,403. In 1827 the building, which was the most modern at the time with 164 cells, was completed, and the total cost was £63,335.5s.6d. (£63,335.27p).

1880 — A mortuary was placed in the gaol, and disinfecting apparatus was installed.

The 1756 building measured 126 feet by 121 feet with two parts — one for felons and the other for Debtors and House of Correction prisoners. The night cells measured 7 feet by 7 feet 4 inches wide and were 8 feet 3 inches high. Rarely were there less than three people to a cell. The new Derby Goal (built in 1827) occupied a six acre site just off Uttoxeter Old Road and had 164 cells. The building still stands today and now serves as the Derby Greyhound Stadium.

BRANDING

In the 17th Century it was possible for a man convicted of a crime to gain exemption by claiming "Benefit of Clergy". He could only do this once. If he could prove to the Court that he could read, he was regarded as a clerk and would be let off the sentence. To ensure that it was claimed only once, the person was branded with a red hot iron in Court, on the left hand. Taken from the Session records of 1696 is the following entry:-

"Whereas John Palmer late of Wirksworth in this County,
butcher indicted at this p'sent Sessions for the felonious
Stealinge of another Sheep price five shillings the goods
and chattells of a p'son Unknowne upon which Indictment
the said John Palmer was arraigned and upon his arrainmt
pleaded not guilty and for his tryall put himselfe upon
his county whoe found him guilty of the felony whereof hee
Stood indicted as aforesaid, whereupon the said John Palmer
prayed the benefit of his clery which was granted him by
the Court, and hee read, whereupon the Court gave judgment
that the said John Palmer should bee burnt in his left hand
which was Executed accordingly."

In 1698, instead of branding on the left hand, persons claiming "Benefit of Clergy" were branded on the left cheek. At the Lent
Assizes in Derby, 1699, two men were branded on the cheek. Seven years later the Act was repealed, since it encouraged bravado and also meant that branders found it hard to obtain a job, leaving them no alternative but to resort to crime. Branding was completely abolished in 1822.

BELVOIR CASTLE — the "witches" lived nearby.

WITCHCRAFT

James the First was the most superstitious man to rule the kingdom — from 1603 to 1625. Before ever coming to the throne, he wrote a book on witchcraft called "Demonologie". Shortly after becoming a king he had an Act passed — "Against Conjuration, Witchcraft and Dealing with Evil and Wicked Spirits". As a result of this, anyone who practised witchcraft, cast spells or did evil things could expect, if arrested, to be put to death. Consequently witch hunting was a popular sport, and it is believed that over 3,000 supposed witches were executed during his reign. The Act was abolished in 1736.

As we have seen in "Burning to Death", Ann Wragg was thus sentenced for being a supposed witch in 1650. Possibly one of the most famous cases in England was the Belvoir Witches, who were executed at Lincoln on 11th March, 1618. Here in Derbyshire there seems to have been very little witchcraft, and the principal case was The Bakewell Witches. Recorded for the year 1608 is the following entry —

"The old Countess of Shrewsbury died about Candlemas....
whose funeral was about Holy Thursday. A great frost
this year. The witches of Bakewell hanged."

This extremely sad story of The Bakewell Witches, which is typical of the period, seems to be thus. A pedlar had been staying at Mrs. Stafford's, who ran a boarding house in Bakewell. He stayed a long time, and had no money to pay for his board. In the end, Mrs. Stafford took his clothes and threw him out in only his nightshirt. He was arrested by a Constable, who had him brought before a magistrate.

To save his own skin, the pedlar concocted the following story....

He was staying at Mrs. Stafford's when one night, in the early hours of the morning, he saw a chink of light shining up through the floorboards. He climbed out of bed and peered through the crack. In the room below he could see Mrs. Stafford and her sister preparing to go out. When they were ready, Mrs. Stafford said —

"Over thick, over thin,
Now Devil, to the cellar in Lunnum." (London?)

At this the lights went out and there was a whoosh of air and they both disappeared. The pedlar went back to bed and pondered over what he had seen. As he did so he said the verse to himself. Whereupon the bedclothes fell off the bed, the windows opened, and he flew through the air and landed in the cellar where Mrs. Stafford and her sister were. They gave him a drink, and he fell instantly asleep, and it was not until the Constable came that he woke up. The Magistrate believed his story and, to add fuel to the fire, his clothes were found at Mrs. Stafford's house. The women were brought to trial, and although they protested their innocence they were hanged soon afterwards.

TRANSPORTATION

Following the Statute introduced in George the First's reign in 1718, many criminals were transported to America. Between 1718 and 1772, when the American penal settlements were closed as a result of the American War of Independence, 199 prisoners were sent from Derbyshire. The Court appointed specific Judges who were responsible for arranging the transportation of the criminal. The Judge communicated with a contractor, whose job it was to transport the criminal to America. The Court — on average — gave him between two and three guineas per criminal for this. The contractor had the personal property of the criminal, who was now "his", and in America he sold him to the highest bidder. Naturally the whole process was legalised with papers. The approximate cost of taking eleven prisoners to the docks in Liverpool, a journey of four days, was £21.

Since prisoners could not be transported to America any more, a new penal settlement was established in 1787 at Botany Bay, New South Wales, Australia. In 1840 the settlement was transferred to Tasmania. Between the years 1787 and 1857, when transportation was abolished, 108,715 convicts were transported from Britain; many came from Derbyshire. In 1817 William Eaton incurred expenses totalling £339 for "conveying 42 convicts to Woolwich and Sheerness". These particular criminals were involved in The Pentrich Rebellion, of which the three ringleaders were executed the same year.

The Round House at Curbar, lying on the south side of the village at Grid Ref. SK 2555744 and can only be reached on foot — a right of way to Baslow passes it. The unusual roofed building was used by prisoners in transit.

THE JUDGEMENT OF PENANCE

"That you be taken back to the prison whence you came,
to a low dungeon into which no light can enter; that
you be laid on your back on the bare floor with a cloth
around your loins, but elsewhere naked; that there be
set upon your body a weight of iron as great as you can
bear — and greater; that you have no sustenance, save
on the first day, three morsels of the coarsest bread,
on the second day three draughts of stagnant water,
from the pool nearest to the prison door, on the third,
again three morsels of bread as before and such bread
and such water alternatively from day to day, until you
die."

From Henry the Fourth's reign, 1399 to 1413 onwards, accused persons who
remained mute in the witness box in the Court would be asked three times to
answer a question. If the accused remained silent the Judgement of Penance was
read out, which was the above sentence. A female mute was dealt with in this
manner in Derby in 1665. Just over a hundred years later, in 1772, an Act was
passed stating that, if the accused remained mute, a verdict of guilty was to be
assumed. This was later changed by a further Act in 1827, when the silence of the
accused was taken to mean a plea of not guilty.

PADLEY CHAPEL

20

CAPITAL PUNISHMENT IN DERBYSHIRE — a random list.

Up to 1829 to Sir Robert Peel's Acts, the death penalty was frequently used, but after this it was only sentenced in specific cases. The Criminal Law Consolidation Act of 1861 made the death penalty applicable only to cases of murder or high treason. The scene of an execution was generally attended by a huge crowd. At the execution of the ringleaders of the Pentrich Rebellion in 1817, there was a crowd of 10,000 or more watching the spectacle. From 1868 all the executions were carried out in private.

1341 — Three men who had been executed for robbery with violence were hung in chains on the outskirts of Chapel-en-le-Frith.
A woman and two men, who had murdered one of the King's purveyors, were gibbeted on Ashover Moor, at the top of Slack Quarry.

1578 — Peter Greaves of Bubnell, Thomas Robinson of Wirksworth, Eleanor Wright of Bakewell, Edward Morrys of Chesterfield and Christopher Harrison of Monyash were hung, following the Derby Summer Assizes.

1588 — The Padley Martyrs — Robert Ludlum and Nicholas Garlick and another Roman Catholic priest — Richard Sympson — were hung, drawn and quartered in Derby on the 24th July.

1637 — Following the Assizes at Chesterfield, on 15th and 16th March, five men and one woman were executed at Tapton Bridge.

1723 — A man was hung in Derby after being convicted of horse stealing.

1753 — A man was hung in Derby for sheep stealing. Another man was hung for stealing £5.17s.0d. (£5.85p)

1801 — The following five were hung: two for highway robbery, one for housebreaking and two for sheep stealing.

1815 — Anthony Lingard, who murdered the tollkeeper at Wardlow Mires, was gibbeted close by, after being hung.

1819 — On March 22nd, Hannah Pecking aged sixteen of Litton, hung. Poisoned Jane Grant of Litton by putting poison in a sweet cake.
— On 2nd April, Thomas Hopkinson, aged twenty, from Ashover, was hung in Derby for highway robbery.

1823 — Samuel Chadwick of Crich, on August 22nd., murdered Susanna Sellars with an axe, splitting her head open.

1833 — The first time the new gallows at the new gaol in Derby were used.

1841 — John Towndrow, aged sixty, from Milltown near Ashover, murdered his wife with a hammer and cut her head off before slitting his own throat.

BURNING TO DEATH

Sentence — "To be drawn on an hurdle to the place of execution
on ...., and burned with fire until she be
dead."

This singularly brutal punishment was used several times in Derbyshire. Although principally used for female heretics, such as Joan Waste, it was also used on women who had either committed high or petty treason. From 1790 onwards, hanging was used instead of burning. The Windmill Pit in Derby was the place where this form of execution was carried out.

Some examples:-

1st August, 1556 — Joan Waste, Derbyshire's only female
martyr.
1601 — Female, for poisoning her husband.
1650 — Ann Wragg, from Ilkeston. Was said to have been
a witch, but there is very little information
to substantiate that she was.
1683 — A female who had murdered her employer at Swanwick.
Believed to be the last instance of this punishment
in Derbyshire.

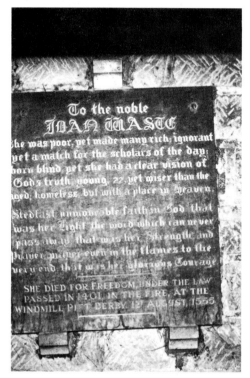

JOAN WASTE PLAQUE, BIRCHOVER CHURCH

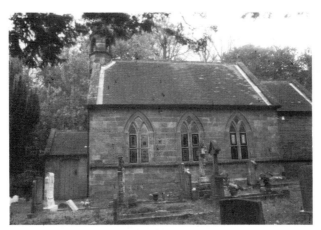

BIRCHOVER CHURCH

JOAN WASTE — DERBYSHIRE'S ONLY FEMALE MARTYR

In Birchover Church, which lies at the southern end of Stanton Moor, can be seen a plaque to Joan Waste. She has no connections with the church, but it is simply a memorial to this sad story, for she was burnt at the stake in Windmill Pit in Derby on 1st August 1556. She was one of 300 Protestants burnt to death during Queen Mary's Catholic reign — 1553 to 1558.

She was born in 1534 in St. Aukmund's Parish of Derby, a twin and blind from birth. Her father, William Waste, was a barber and rope maker. As soon as she was able, she learnt to knit and to turn the wheel for her father as he made ropes. When her parents died she carried on doing this work for her brother, Roger Waste. She lived a quiet and godly life and, having earned sufficient money, she purchased a bible. Friends would read to her and she learned it off by heart. This kind of behaviour was quite acceptable during Edward the Sixth's reign, but when Queen Mary came to the throne the situation was reversed. Word of her Bible reading came to the attention of the Bishop, and she was placed into prison, where other prisoners would read to her.

"These were sufficient reasons in those horrible days for
her to be looked upon with suspicion, seized, cast into
prison, tried by a mock tribunal and burned at the stake."

This is indeed what happened, and at the age of twenty-two she was burnt to death, the only religious female martyr in Derbyshire. Finally, as the plaque in Birchover records —

"Steadfast unmovable faith in God, that was her light, the
word which can never pass away, that was her strength and
prayer, prayer even in the flames to the very end; and
that was her glorious courage."

HUNG, DRAWN AND QUARTERED

"That you and each of you be carried to the place from
whence you came, and from thence be drawn on a hurdle
to the place of execution and be severally hanged but
be cut down while you are alive; that your privy
members be cut off; that your bowels be taken out
and burnt before your faces; that your bodies be
divided into four quarters and that your quarters be
at the Queen's disposal and Lord have mercy on your
souls."

The above sentence was passed on two Roman Catholic priests, who were
arrested at Padley Chapel, near Grindleford Station, on 12th July 1588. The two
priests, Robert Ludlam and Nicholas Garlick, together with another priest,
Richard Sympson, were hung, drawn and quartered at Derby on the 24th July,
1588. Padley Chapel is now a permanent memorial to them, and a plaque to these
Derbyshire martyrs can be seen in St. Mary's Church, Derby. Their arrest and
execution was during a period of history when the Roman Catholic faith in
England was being persecuted by Elizabeth I, who was a Protestant. A pilgrimage
to Padley Chapel is made on the Thursday nearest to 12th July and the following
Sunday, each year.

Another case of this singularly brutal form of execution is the execution of the
three ringleaders of The Pentrich Rebellion in 1817. The Prince Regent signed the
execution authorisation on 1st November 1817, but ruled that the quartering was
not to take place. The three, Jeremiah Brandeth, William Turner and Isaac Ludlam,
were hung until dead before having their heads cut off. The chopping block can
be seen in Derby Museum, along with many other exhibits of former punishments.

ARREST AND EXECUTION WINDOW, PADLEY CHAPEL

REV. RICHARD SYMPSON WINDOW, PADLEY CHAPEL

GIBBETING

This method of humiliation of the parents or relations of the murderer was one of the more distasteful punishments of the 17th, 18th and early 19th Centuries. Very often the murderer was convicted and hung, his body would then be taken to the scene of the murder and hung in chains from a post. Quite often the body was smeared with tar, so that it remained longer at the scene of his crime. A highwayman who had robbed a stagecoach near Duffield in 1750 was thus treated. A few weeks after his body had been gibbeted, his friends set fire to it.

As mentioned in the Capital Punishment section, there were two sets of gibbets in 1341. The last person to be gibbeted at Derby was Mathew Cocayne in 1776. He had murdered Mary Vicars, and he was gibbeted near Tenant Street where she lived. Just east of Chatsworth House is Gibbet Moor. Here was the scene for the last live gibbet in Derbyshire. A tramp was walking nearby, and on reaching a house he forced the woman inside to give him some food. Eventually he lost his temper and began fighting her. When they reached the kitchen he took hold of a pan of hot fat and poured it down her throat, killing her. He was caught three days later and gibbeted alive. The Duke of Devonshire, nearby, could hear him screaming at night. As a result of this, it was the last live gibbet in Derbyshire.

The last gibbet in Derbyshire was at Wardlow Mires. Here in 1815 on 1st April, Anthony Lingard, who had murdered the tollkeeper, Hannah Oliver, there, was gibbeted. He was hung in Derby, and the gaoler charged ten guineas (£10.50p) to transfer his body from the gaol to Wardlow. The cost of the gibbet was £85.4s.0d. (£85.20p). Shortly before a person was hung, he was measured for his "last suit" — the gibbet, as it was called. Often they broke down when this was being done.

WARDLOW MIRES

26

Rhodes, in his "Peak Scenery" (1818), recalls this gibbet. "As we passed the road to Tideswell, the little villages of Wardlow and Litton lay on our left.....here, at a little distance on the left of the road, we observed a man suspended on a gibbet, which was but newly erected."

The gibbet was taken down on April 10th 1826 and the remains of Lingard were buried on the site.

William Newton, better known as the Minstrel of the Peak, wrote a poem on this gibbet, and, although he died before he saw it happen, his poem was largely responsible for the abolition of gibbeting in 1834.

Extracts from Newton's poem — "The supposed soliloquy of a Father under the Gibbet of his son, upon one of the Peak Mountains near Wardlow." Time: Midnight. Scene: A Storm.

"Art thou, my son, suspended here on high, —
Ah! what a sight to meet a Father's eye!
To see what most I prized, what most I loved,
What most I cherised, — and once approved,
Hung in mid air to feed the nauseous worm,
And waving horrid in the midnight storm!

My Son! My Son! how dreadful was thy crime!
Thy name stands branded to remotest time;

If crime demand it, let the offender die,
But let no more the Gibbet brave the sky;
No more let vengeance on the dead be hurl'd,
But hide the victim from a gazing world."

MINSTREL OF THE PEAK — WILLIAM NEWTON'S GRAVE, TIDESWELL CHURCH

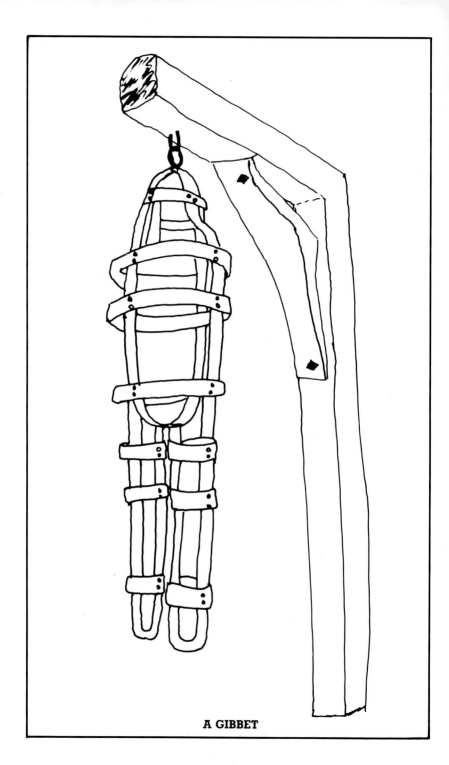

A GIBBET

OTHER BOOKS BY JOHN N. MERRILL PUBLISHED BY JNM PUBLICATIONS

DAY WALK GUIDES —

SHORT CIRCULAR WALKS IN THE PEAK DISTRICT
LONG CIRCULAR WALKS IN THE PEAK DISTRICT
CIRCULAR WALKS IN WESTERN PEAKLAND
SHORT CIRCULAR WALKS IN THE STAFFORDSHIRE MOORLANDS
PEAK DISTRICT TOWN WALKS
SHORT CIRCULAR WALKS AROUND MATLOCK
SHORT CIRCULAR WALKS IN THE DUKERIES
SHORT CIRCULAR WALKS IN SOUTH YORKSHIRE
SHORT CIRCULAR WALKS AROUND DERBY
SHORT CIRCULAR WALKS AROUND BUXTON
SHORT CIRCULAR WALKS AROUND NOTTINGHAMSHIRE
SHORT CIRCULAR WALKS ON THE NORTHERN MOORS
40 SHORT CIRCULAR PEAK DISTRICT WALKS
SHORT CIRCULAR WALKS IN THE HOPE VALLEY

INSTRUCTION & RECORD —

HIKE TO BE FIT....STROLLING WITH JOHN
THE JOHN MERRILL WALK RECORD BOOK

CANAL WALK GUIDES —

VOL ONE — DERBYSHIRE AND NOTTINGHAMSHIRE
VOL TWO — CHESHIRE AND STAFFORDSHIRE
VOL THREE — STAFFORDSHIRE
VOL FOUR — THE CHESHIRE RING

DAY CHALLENGE WALKS —

JOHN MERRILL'S PEAK DISTRICT CHALLENGE WALK
JOHN MERRILL'S YORKSHIRE DALES CHALLENGE WALK
JOHN MERRILL'S NORTH YORKSHIRE MOORS CHALLENGE WALK
PEAK DISTRICT END TO END WALKS
THE LITTLE JOHN CHALLENGE WALK
JOHN MERRILL'S LAKELAND CHALLENGE WALK
JOHN MERRILL'S STAFFORDSHIRE MOORLAND CHALLENGE WALK
JOHN MERRILL'S DARK PEAK CHALLENGE WALK

MULTIPLE DAY WALKS —

THE RIVERS' WAY
PEAK DISTRICT HIGH LEVEL ROUTE

PEAK DISTRICT MARATHONS
THE LIMEY WAY
THE PEAKLAND WAY

COAST WALKS —

ISLE OF WIGHT COAST WALK
PEMBROKESHIRE COAST PATH
THE CLEVELAND WAY

HISTORICAL GUIDES —

DERBYSHIRE INNS
HALLS AND CASTLES OF THE PEAK DISTRICT & DERBYSHIRE
TOURING THE PEAK DISTRICT AND DERBYSHIRE BY CAR
DERBYSHIRE FOLKLORE
LOST INDUSTRIES OF DERBYSHIRE
PUNISHMENT IN DERBYSHIRE
CUSTOMS OF THE PEAK DISTRICT AND DERBYSHIRE
WINSTER — A VISITOR'S GUIDE
ARKWRIGHT OF CROMFORD
TALES FROM THE MINES by GEOFFREY CARR

JOHN'S MARATHON WALKS —

TURN RIGHT AT LAND'S END
WITH MUSTARD ON MY BACK
TURN RIGHT AT DEATH VALLEY
EMERALD COAST WALK

COLOUR GUIDES —

THE PEAK DISTRICT . . . Something to remember her by.

SKETCH BOOKS — by John Creber

NORTH STAFFORDSHIRE SKETCHBOOK